Vegetaria Beginners

50 Delicious Recipes And 8 Weeks Of Diet Plans

By Jessica Brooks

The trademarks that are used are without any consent, and the publication of the trademark is without permission or backing by the trademark owner. All trademarks and brands within this book are for clarifying purposes only and are the owned by the owners themselves, not affiliated with this document.

Disclaimer – Please read!

The information provided in this book is designed to provide helpful information on the subjects discussed. This book is not meant to be used, nor should it be used, to diagnose or treat any medical condition. For diagnosis or treatment of any medical problem, consult your own physician. The publisher and author are not responsible for any specific health or allergy needs that may require medical supervision and are not liable for any damages or negative consequences from any treatment, action, application or preparation, to any person reading or following the information in this book. References are provided for informational purposes only and do not constitute endorsement of any websites or other sources. Readers should be aware that the websites listed in this book may change.

Table Of Contents

Chapter Five: 10 Lunch Recipes

Chapter Six: 10 Dinnertime Recipes

Chapter Seven: 10 Snack Recipes

Chapter Eight: 10 Sauce, Dip and Condiments Recipes

Conclusion
Free Ebook Offer
About the Author
Valerian Press

Introduction

The vegetarian diet can be quite a daunting prospect for anyone new to the idea, it can after all be quite a massive lifestyle change. This book is the perfect introduction to the world of vegetarianism! Whether you are simply moving from a Mediterranean to a vegetarian diet, or transferring from a standard diet rich in meat and animal products this book will guide you happily through the process. I will provide a bit of background on the vegetarian diet, explaining the history of how it came to be such a large and important movement today. You'll find out exactly what the diet entails and learn about the huge range of health benefits that come with it. I'll teach you how to make the changes required, ranging from shopping guides, dealing with eating out, dealing with cravings and provide you with a list of approved foods. After all the learning is out of the way you'll be provided with two four-week diet plans, with the recipes for many of the meals included in the later chapters. The 50 recipes include 10 for breakfast, lunch and dinner. 10 snack recipes and also 10 recipes for making vegetarian sauces and condiments!

There is no presumed knowledge at all, that is, even if you know absolutely nothing about vegetarianism you will not feel lost or overwhelmed at any point in this book. However, you can feel confident that by the time you have finished this book you will be more than capable of beginning your vegan diet to improve the health of yourself and your family.

The health benefits that come from eating a good vegetarian diet are simply stunning. You will be eating a large variety of the most nutritious, vitamin and mineral dense foods on the planet. You will start to feel more energetic and vitalized than before, your skin will appear healthier and your overall outlook on life will improve. So let's get started!

Thanks for choosing this book. I hope it both inspires you and answers all the questions you have.

Chapter One: Understanding Vegetarianism

Vegetarianism has enjoyed a diverse history, which has been preserved throughout many cultures since the dawn of time. Vegetarianism was popular among some of the greatest figures in the classical world, particularly Pythagoras in 580 BC. This independent thinker was the first to admit that animals needed to be treated well and that people should abstain from eating meat. His ideas mirrored traditions from earlier civilizations such as the Ancient Egyptians. There was a vegetarian ideology practiced in 3200 BC among religious groups in Egypt who not only abstained from eating animals, but also abstained from wearing clothing derived from animals. Their belief in reincarnation was the key influence on this decision.

Among the Greek traditions of Pythagoras, it was expected to avoid animal cruelty but also to enjoy the health benefits that a diet free from animal flesh brings. Pythagoras viewed vegetarianism as one of the key factors to creating coexistence among people. His idea was that the slaughtering of animals caused the human soul to be brutalized. Many other Ancient Greek speakers who came after him believed in his way of thinking, and worked in favor of a vegetarian diet for most of their lives.

Theophrastus was a student of Aristotle who succeeded him as the leader of the Lyceum in Athens. He supported the vegetarian diet. Socrates and Plato debated the status of animals and whether they were equal to slaves or not. Unfortunately, Pythagoras found limited support within Ancient Rome due to the high rate of wild animals being murdered in Gladiator games.

Many followers of vegetarianism at the time were fearful of persecution, and coined the term Pythagorean to mean vegetarian. This term was used to communicate with other vegetarians throughout Ancient Rome between the third and sixth century without being seen as a subversive. Plutarch included an essay on eating animal flesh and why you should abstain from animal foods. Apollinaris was a strict vegetarian who spoke out against grain restrictions, among other things.

Throughout Asia, abstinence from animal meat was a key concept within many religious philosophies, including Hinduism, Jainism, Zoroastrianism, and Brahinanism. There are ancient verses among the sacred Hindu texts which encourage vegetarianism, and the doctrines of respect for all life is pivotal after the other mentioned religions. Vegetarianism has been a key concept among Buddhism, a belief system which enshrines total compassion for every living thing. The King of India, who converted to Buddhism in 264 BC, was shocked by the true horror of war. He turned his kingdom into a vegetarian kingdom, and animal sacrifices were put to an end.

In early Christianity, while many people believed that humans were supreme over slaves and animals, a few unorthodox groups continued to practice vegetarianism within their belief structures. Between the third and eighth centuries, the main philosophy was against animal slaughter, and yet these nonviolent vegetarians were seen as fanatics, feared and persecuted by the Christian Church.

Bogomilsis is a vegetarian sect which currently resides in Bulgaria. Between the third and 10th century A.D., they were burned at the stake for hearsay. Unfortunately in Medieval Europe during the 10th century, the anti-heretic movement took precedence throughout most of Europe, with many people killed. However, St. Francis of Assisi, and Saint David, the Patron Saint of Wales, were both notable vegetarians who managed to escape the fervor during the 10th century.

During the beginning of the Renaissance, vegetarian ideology was rare. Famine was everywhere as crops began to fail, and food began to fall short. Meat was a luxury reserved for the rich. The ancient philosophy of vegetarianism began to influence people throughout Europe. Classical writers such as Pythagoras were rediscovered, and the idea that animals were sensitive to pain the same way humans were, and therefore were themselves human. Thus to eat animals was foregoing a moral consideration. This idea began to spread throughout Europe as a popular point of view. It was the opposite view to the new scientific method. As new lands were conquered and new vegetables were introduced throughout Europe - including maize, potatoes and cauliflower - the population's health began to improve. Skin diseases, which up until that point had been widespread, began to diminish.

Cornaro was a well-known dietitian who criticized the excess of the wealthy upper-class in Italy and promoted the vegetarian diet. Thomas Moore wrote about the plight of animals and the brutal practices associated with killing them for meat. Leonardo da Vinci was repulsed by slaughtering animals, and was one of the few during that time to openly denounce meat consumption.

During the 18th-century, as the Enlightenment grew, people began to rethink the place of people among both creation and the animal kingdom. Descartes tried to scientifically disprove that animals have souls, and that they were instead a machine, but it was Thomas Lock opposite him who argued that animals were in fact intelligent and that they could feel pain when mistreated. Soon the idea that consuming flesh of animals was inhumane re-emerged, but not for very long. The killing of animals for meat became a barbaric practice for a long period of time, under the idea that God willed people to eat animals.

During this time, there were very few vegetarians, yet some were quite popular. These included John Gay, the English? Royal physician, John Howard, John Wesley and Alexander Pope. John Wesley started the Methodist movement, influenced by a former physician who had adopted the vegetarian diet to cure himself of his obesity and addictions in the 18th century. This doctor wrote about the direct impact that changing his diet had on his health. In later years, philosophers like Russo and Voltaire would criticize and critique the inhumanity those animals were given. While they were not vegetarians themselves, they did raise the plight of animals as a key issue among people.

In the 19th century, reform was taking place. Humanist reform emerged alongside romantic spiritualism and religious reforms. William Lambe was a popular figure in both the medical and literary world in regards to the vegetarian diet. Radical thinkers and poets, alongside Dr. John Newton, promoted the vegetarian diet. This would become the foundation for the current vegetarian society.

The poet Shelley declared himself vegetarian in 1812 due to the health advantages of avoiding the consumption of meat. He also added that food shortages took place among the lower classes as a result of meat production and an overall inefficient use of current resources. This political ideology helped to bring vegetarianism out of the shadows.

In 1809, an offshoot among the Church of England began to work toward vegetarianism, with biblical references used against the consumption of meat. Reverend William Cowherd established the Vegetarian Society in 1809, and the congregation enjoyed improved healing and overall better health. They were also all vegetarians. William Metcalfe fled to Philadelphia from the English Crown in 1817, and in 1850 he set up the American Vegetarian Society.

The influence that these vegetarian churches had throughout the 19th century was grand. Large congregations of poor believers began to join fundamentalist Christian groups who were vegetarian. In America as well as Britain, many people began to practice vegetarianism. Vegetarian communes were evident as early as the 1830s. Dr. John Harvey Kellogg was a popular preacher of the vegetarian radical Christianity belief system, and he was also the inventor of the now famous breakfast cereals. It was in 1880 that vegetarian restaurants began to open throughout London. They provided inexpensive, nutritious meals in a formal, more respectable setting.

By the 20th century, the health rates and levels of poverty and infant mortality in Britain were still significant. The Vegetarian Society was formed in its entirety and began to send food parcels into the mining communities in 1926, during the general strikes. And at the same time, vegetarianism was gaining more publicity due to Mahatma Gandhi, who wrote extensively on the subject and made vegetarianism a key part of his life.

In the Second World War, the British were encouraged to grow fruits and vegetables under the slogan "Dig for Victory". Many people sustained a vegetarian diet during this time simply because of ongoing food rations, and yet their health greatly improved. Vegetarians during the Second World War were given unique ration cards which allowed them to consume more eggs, cheese, and nuts. During 1945 in the United Kingdom, there were over 100,000 vegetarians. Today, there over 2 million.

During the 1950s and 1960s, factory farming and animal hoarders became prominent in the media. In America, the movement lagged a bit due to the prevalent development of television dinners, frozen dinners, and fast food restaurants.

Soon vegetarianism became a counterculture once again, and in the 1970s the movement was given significant academic attention when Peter Singer authored the book "Animal Liberation Against the Ethics of Animal Welfare".

As environmental issues clouded the headlines between the 1970s and 1990s, vegetarianism was more sincerely considered by the masses because of the otherwise disastrous impact that meat production was having on the Earth. Vegetarianism was seen as a way to conserve current resources. In the early 2000s, many infectious diseases, transmitted only via improper meat consumption began to rise and this increased attention towards the idea of vegetarianism.

The history of vegetarianism is incredibly diverse in both its characters and events. It has been evident in cultures all over the world, and has sustained people for thousands of years.

Whether you choose to be vegetarian for economic, religious, or moral reasons, vegetarianism shows many benefits to health and environment, and you will have the support of the world behind you.

The health benefits

Vegetarianism is a healthier choice. Vegetarian diets are low in fat, particularly saturated fat. A balanced diet is full of fruits and vegetables, which makes it high in complex carbohydrates. When many people hear the term "carbohydrates", they misunderstand. There are two types of carbohydrates, which are found in nearly every food we consume, including fruits and vegetables: simple and complex carbohydrates. Simple carbohydrates are, as their name would suggest, simple. Your body can break them down immediately, which is what gives you the energy high following consumption of foods such as white bread or pasta. However, with that high comes an immediate drop in blood sugar levels. You encourage the immediate spike of insulin, and consequently an immediate drop when you consume too many simple carbohydrates. This is what causes people to feel initially excited and then incredibly fatigued. A constant influx and decrease of your insulin levels is unhealthy for your body.

Complex carbohydrates are those typically found in fruits and vegetables, which take a bit longer to break down, and therefore do not cause a spike in insulin, instead a slow distribution of energy and sugar levels. This is significantly healthier for your body.

When you convert to vegetarianism, you cut out a lot of the fat from your diet. Meat does provide a lot of animal-based protein, though you can consume almost all of your proteins from plant sources, but it also provides a lot of fat, saturated fat in particular. By cutting meat from your diet, you replace a lot of the bad fat that comes with it, with better fats. This can help reduce your rate of heart disease and lower your chance of salmonella poisoning.

The rate of food poisoning, which affects millions of people every year, is generally from the consumption of spoiled meat, which has not properly stored, prepared, or cooked properly. Those who cut meat out from their diet alleviate this risk.

The dietary change also helps with weight loss. Many people struggle today with losing weight, unable to cut those extra pounds. But eating unhealthy foods like pizza, chips, French fries, and downing it all with a Coke makes it incredibly difficult to lose weight. And yet studies indicate that most vegetarians are slimmer and healthier than meat eaters. So if you want to lose weight, converting to vegetarianism might be a good part of your program. And in general, vegetarians replace a lot of their meat with more nutritious foods, including beans, vegetables, whole grains and fruit. This allows them to get more of the nutrients that their body needs and leaves you better, healthier, and with more energy.

Research indicates vegetarians are significantly less likely to suffer from diseases such as type two diabetes, obesity, high blood pressure, coronary heart disease, and diet-related cancers. Vegetarianism brings with it a higher portion of fruits and vegetables each day, something that many people who eat meat fail to achieve.

But vegetarianism does not just bring with it health benefits, it also brings with it compassion for animals and a better environmental footprint, one which encourages sustainability, protects the oceans, and saves water and land. Livestock actually causes more pollution than the whole of the transportation system today. Keeping farm animals hydrated consumes more of the world's freshwater resources than people. This is why eating a vegetarian diet helps to protect the world from harmful greenhouse gases, and save land and water.

Turning to the vegetarian diet brings with it profound benefits for your overall well-being. So let's get into how you can reap the many benefits by converting today...

Chapter Two: Starting Your Diet

15 helpful tips for starting a vegetarian diet

For those of you who are making the transition to vegetarianism, below are 15 tips to help you successfully begin the change:

1. You want to have a good reason. Don't just become a vegetarian because. If you don't have a good reason for becoming a vegetarian, you won't stick with it when it's difficult. Vegetarianism is not just a quick fix, but a lifestyle change. And as with any lifestyle change, it requires motivation to really think about why you want to become a vegetarian, and actually believe in it. If you have strong convictions for becoming a vegetarian, chances are you will stick with it.

2. You should do your homework. Read up about vegetarianism before you start. Read over different cookbooks, and review websites and books about the topic. Before you start anything new, you should do a lot of research and know a lot about it.

3. Find great recipes. You don't have to buy a ton of new cookbooks; you can always look online for great vegetarian forums or ask your vegetarian friends if you can borrow their cookbooks. At first it can be a bit overwhelming, so just look at a few recipes and take note of the ones that you like. You can even begin to integrate vegetarianism slowly, substituting three or four meals per week with a vegetarian option. Test it out and see if it works for you.

4. Try using substitutes in your cooking. If you love spaghetti or chili, use alternatives for ground beef and see how the meal fares. Use a meatless option for the things that you would normally eat, and soon enough you won't notice the difference.

5. One of the easiest ways to transition into vegetarianism is to

begin with red meat. You don't have to give up all meat at the same time. Try one or two vegetarian meals for your first week, and then two or three vegetarian meals for your second week.

Start by alleviating red meat. Remove red meat from your diet, and try to focus more on white meat only. Then begin to cut out pork. A few weeks after that, start to cut out chicken. A few weeks after that, cut out seafood. This approach will make it significantly easier for you to transition into vegetarianism without really noticing that you've done it.

6. Think about dairy products and eggs. You can cut them out of your diet, or you can choose to keep them in your diet. Choice is really yours. Vegetarians do both. See what feels right for you. If you can go meatless for a few months but you can't give up your cheese topping or your egg omelet in the morning, that's perfectly fine.

7. Think about the staple items. One useful exercise when transitioning to vegetarianism is to make a list of the foods that you would normally eat for breakfast, lunch, dinner, and snacks. Don't list the meals, list the ingredients and then think about what vegetarian alternatives you can use. For example, if you eat chicken stir-fry for dinner, try tofu stir-fry for dinner. You will begin to create a new list of staple items and replace what you have in your pantry with these vegetarian-friendly staples.

8. Make sure that you get enough protein. Remember that the idea of not getting enough protein as a vegetarian is false. But you do need to get a varied diet in order to get the protein that you need. This is why the stereotype that vegetarians only eat lettuce is also a myth. Having a varied diet, which includes soy protein, nuts, grains, beans and vegetables, will help ensure you get adequate protein. You can get a high dose of plant-based protein, and you will be just fine. So make sure that your meals are varied.

9. Try ethnic foods. Becoming a vegetarian will often spur a new love of ethnic food. There are many vegetarian dishes that

are popular all over the world, including Thai, Mexican, Italian and Indian food. You can try to do different things for different nights of the week, such as Italian nights, or Mexican night, and sample ethnic foods from around the world.

10. Plan ahead. If you are going out to eat or you're going to a party, ask the host if you can prepare a dish and bring it. If you know that the dinner party will be meat-heavy, eat before you go.

11. Cook ahead of time. There are not many vegetarian foods that are instantaneous. This is what often leads people to crave fast food. If you are incredibly hungry as soon as you come home, it can be challenging to prepare a vegetarian meal because it takes a lot of time.

You can create a vegetarian lasagna or a vegetarian chili and keep it in your freezer for those nights that you are incredibly hungry and need something immediately. This will help to alleviate the risk of falling back on an unhealthy snack option.

12. Try vegetarian snacks. Make fruit or vegetable cups. Have roasted almonds and hummus on hand. Keep whole-grain cereals and crackers on hand so that you can make quick and healthy snack plates in between meals.

13. Have fun. If you make becoming a vegetarian a restrictive ordeal, you will feel deprived and not want to continue. It should be something that's fun. Test different foods and see what you can find. Find menu and recipe options that you enjoy. This should be a great endeavor that brings you happiness.

14. Tell your friends and family that you are becoming vegetarian. If you let them know at social gatherings or group dinners they might be more inclined to prepare a vegetarian dish just for you the next time you come over. Be open and informative about your choice, but do not get argumentative or defensive. If you start a fight with people, they will no longer be receptive and they will more than likely write off the concept of vegetarianism as a whole. But if you can be open

and tell people what you're doing and why, they might be willing to try it themselves.

15. Remember that no lifestyle choice you make is necessarily the right lifestyle choice for someone else. Never force your ideas on to those around you.

Shopping Guide

When you shop as a vegetarian, your choices are not nearly as constricted as you might believe.

When you are shopping as a vegetarian, it is best to stick to the perimeter of any commercial grocery store. Commercial stores are laid out with the fresh produce along the perimeter and less healthy and frozen items in the center. In the center is where you can find staple pantry items, but for fresh produce, stick to the outside. If you can, shop at local farmers' markets and nearby co-ops for fresh, organic, local food.

Food Items

As a vegetarian, there are a few staple items that you should have in your pantry at all times. Whether you are new to the vegetarian diet or you just want to integrate a lot of healthier ingredients into your life, there are many things that you should have on hand at all times. Fresh produce is a staple item, but it is also something that you have to purchase regularly and keep stocked in your fridge. Produce should be as fresh as possible and sticking with what is in season helps to not only support family farms, but helps you to enjoy organic produce. Things you should keep stored in your refrigerators are just one of the two elements you need to keep on hand. You also need to keep your pantry stocked.

It is good to search for jarred or canned beans from your favorite farmers markets or co-ops that have no additives. You should include:

- Black beans
- Black-eyed peas
- Kidney beans
- Garbanzo beans
- Cannellini beans
- Pinto beans
- Pink beans

If you want to cook beans from scratch, that is even better. All of these beans are better when they're cooked from scratch, and you can incorporate large amounts of them in conjunction with lentils and split peas. Be advised that making beans from scratch does require you plan the day ahead and leave your beans soaking overnight in almost every case.

Whole grains and whole wheat flour should also be kept on hand, but keep them at room temperature and never buy more than you will consume within the span of three months. If it is incredibly hot in the summer, refrigerate these items. You should have in your pantry:

- Barley
- Couscous
- Quinoa
- Brown and wild rice
- Whole-grain berries
- Cornmeal
- Specialty whole-wheat flour
- Specialty rice flour

It is good for you to keep a range of herbs and spices on hand in their dried form. Having dried powders and spices on hand can help make it incredibly easy to liven up any dish you are preparing. If you can have fresh herbs and spices, that is great, however you may not always be able to have them when you need them and that is when dried substitutes are ideal.

You also want to keep a few oils on hand, including:

- Coconut oil
- Sunflower oil
- Extra-virgin olive oil
- Dark sesame oil

You should have a handful of pasta in your pantry, including whole wheat angel hair pasta, fettuccine, linguine, and spirals. You can also have Asian noodles on hand, such as rice noodles.

It is good for you to have nuts and seeds as well as nut butter. Keep peanuts, walnuts, pumpkin seeds, almonds, cashews, sesame seeds, and pecans on hand. If you keep Chia seeds or flaxseeds, they need to be refrigerated. You can also keep organic nut butter on hand such as almond butter or cashew butter. If you have a strong enough blender, you can make these things at home. It is also best to have soy sauce on hand to add flavor in a natural way. You should keep canned tomato products in your pantry, including cans of diced tomatoes and tomato sauce. It is good to have organic apple cider vinegar, rice vinegar, red wine vinegar and balsamic vinegar on hand for cooking. In terms of condiments and sauces, it is good to have a natural marinara sauce, salad dressings, salsa, stir-fry sauce, and Thai peanut sauce. In terms of pantry vegetables, you should keep potatoes, onions, garlic, sweet potatoes, and silken tofu on hand.

In addition to all of this, you should purchase fresh produce based on the things you want to cook. Remember to plan regular trips to the store for the freshest items. While it might seem like a lot of invested time, there are services today throughout Europe and America which deliver fresh produce on a weekly basis to your home. You can benefit greatly from utilizing such a service, and it can cut down on the majority of your shopping trips.

Eating Out

Stereotypes about vegetarians would lead you to believe that they only eat a piece of lettuce. But this is far from the truth. Just because vegetarians do not eat animals does not mean that their diets are unbalanced or boring.

Eating out at non-vegetarian restaurants can be difficult, but not impossible. If you have family or friends amenable to your suggestions, you can always ask to try a new vegetarian restaurant once in a while, or try a vegetarian-friendly restaurant. Many people who consume meat are surprised at how vegetarian dishes are prepared, and how many non-vegetarian restaurants will offer a vegetarian alternative. Many international-based cuisines, including Greek, Thai, Indian and Chinese restaurants, will have vegetarian dishes on the menu.

If they do not list a vegetarian option on the menu, there are still things you can do. You can ask for a regular dish to be converted into a vegetarian-friendly dish. For example, in an Asian restaurant you might ask that the oyster sauce be exchanged for something else or removed entirely. If you are in an Asian restaurant and they have a chicken curry on the menu, you can simply ask for the chicken to be withheld, making it a vegetable heavy curry delight.

If you know that your friends or family will be heading to a new restaurant in the near future, you can do your research before you go. Call the restaurant to see if they have vegetarian options. They might have copies of their menu on the restaurant website. If they do, you can look up the menu and see what options they have. You can plan ahead by reviewing what options can be most easily converted into a vegetarian-friendly option. If you want to be extra sure, you can call the restaurant and let them know when you will be arriving, and ask if they can convert your dish for you. Sometimes you need to speak with the chef who is currently cooking to get a good answer. If you call the day you are going to visit and ask, for example, if the chicken curry can be converted into a chicken-free curry to meet your vegetarian needs, he might be happy to oblige.

Worst case scenario, your friends pick a meat-heavy barbecue joint and you can simply order a handful of side dishes. Even places like outback steakhouses have wonderful vegetarian side dishes, including a range of potatoes, broccoli, salad, corn, and many other things. If you go to a place like this, you can simply ask for 3 to 5 side dishes to complete your meal. And if none of these methods will work - you're going to a restaurant that has no side dishes and is unwilling to compromise - you can simply eat ahead of time. No one will fault you for eating ahead of time, showing up at the restaurant, and then consuming a wonderful mixed drink.

The Truth about Your Food

One of the few things that people fail to recognize with their diet is that not everything they are told to believe in commercials is true. Many people, for example, believe that they could not give up dairy products like milk because they absolutely need milk to get vitamin D. But many people do not realize that the consumption of milk causes high acidity in the body, which means the body must bring balance back by leaching calcium from the bones. Therefore, high amounts of animal-based milk are not as healthy as we are led to believe. This is due to an inaccurate understanding of alkaline and acidic contents in the body, something which vegetarian diets can naturally rectify.

What is Alkalizing?

In order to understand the process of alkalizing your body, you need to look at two extremes of the same spectrum. On one end, you have alkalizing. On the other end you have acidic. You might remember something about this from your high school science course.

There are some substances which are neither acidic nor alkalizing, and they are called neutral. Just like in science class, the pH scale is used to measure how alkalizing or acidic a substance might be. The pH scale ranges between 0 and 14. A pH balance that is higher than 7 is considered alkalizing, while a pH balance that is lower than 7 is acidic. Something that is actually 7 is neutral. pH actually stands for "potential hydrogen". That means pH measures the amount of electrical resistance between negative and positive ions in your body. Positive ions form acid, while negative ions are alkalizing. So, in essence, the pH measurement reviews how ions push against each other.

But how much should your body have? How much alkalizing do you need? Well, in order to maintain the best body, you want to keep a pH level near 7.4. This means it is slightly alkalizing. But an acceptable range fluctuates between 7.36 and 7.44. In order for your body to run at maximum capacity, and for blood to work effectively, the pH must remain within this range so that you get all of the vital nutrients and oxygen you need into your bloodstream. If you deviate too far from this perfect balance, it can be quite harmful. Most Americans do not realize that the average diet is highly acidic and therefore they need alkalizing. The body has natural alkaline reserves and will do its best to re-balance any fluctuation in your pH levels. However, a reserve is limited and in order to restore it, you must consume foods and juices that are alkalizing.

Why do people become overly acidic?

It is not just diet that can cause an imbalance in our pH levels. The body creates acid that needs to be neutralized when we breathe, digest food, and use certain muscles. That's not to say that diet does not play a role. Diets full of refined foods, grains, processed foods, carbohydrates, and sugars can all increase acid. The average American consumes twice the amount of acid their body can handle. Without alkalizing the body, it cannot get the vitamins and minerals it needs to neutralize this acid.

A lack of alkalizing can cause serious health complications. Too much acid will cause the body to take substances from the vital tissues or bones that it cannot find elsewhere in order to counter it. This impairs your body's ability to repair itself causing you to become more susceptible to diseases and illnesses. If you do not alkalize your body, it can lead to other negative effects, including:

- Joint paint
- Indigestion
- Headaches
- Acne
- Weak hair and nails
- Difficulty gaining or losing weight
- Allergies
- Low immune system

More serious complications can include the cultivation of bacteria and yeast, as well as cancer cells. All major organs and glands can be influenced by a bad pH balance including your thyroid, pancreas, liver, heart, lungs, kidney, and colon.

Thankfully, there are alkalizing foods, just as there are acidic foods. You can consume more fresh fruits and vegetables to help alkalize your body. Lemons squeezed in warm water are a great way to help alkalize your body. Leafy greens like Swiss chard, kale, and spinach are full of the phytochemicals, antioxidants, and vitamins and minerals that your body needs to restore balance. Root vegetables like radishes, carrots, beets, and turnips are all incredibly alkalizing. Cucumbers will quickly neutralize acids in your body and help digestion, as will celery. Garlic is highly alkalizing, and also provides your immune system with a great boost. In addition to these benefits, raw garlic acts as an anti-fungal and antibacterial agent. Avocadoes are not only a great source of omega-3 fatty acid, but they have a high amount of amino acids and vitamins, which will help to alkalize your body. You can also consume cruciferous vegetables like broccoli and cabbage.

Below you will find some charts to help you make better food and drink choices in an effort to alkaline your body.

A list of highly alkaline items:

- Alfalfa
- Celery
- Peppers
- Broccoli
- Cabbage
- Greens
- Chlorella
- Onions
- Cucumber
- Dulce
- Green beans
- Garlic
- Lettuce
- Kale
- Pumpkin
- Edible flowers
- Wild greens
- Watercress
- Wheat grass
- Kohlrabi
- Dandelions
- Spirulina

Here is a list of highly acidic items:

- Beef
- Ice cream
- Canned fruits
- Ice milk
- Peanuts
- Bacon
- Tuna
- Corn
- Sugar
- Vinegar

- Corn syrup
- Cereals
- Mustard
- Mayonnaise
- Corn tortillas
- Milk
- Sardines
- Soft drinks
- Halva
- Artificial sweeteners
- Ketchup

Of course each item has its degree of acidity or alkalinity. If 7 is neutral on the pH scale and 10 is highly alkaline while 2 is highly acidic then follow the list of food items below:

3: Carbonated water, club soda, energy drinks.

4: Popcorn, buttermilk, pastries, pasta, cheese, pork, black tea, beer, wine, cream cheese, prunes, chocolate, roasted nuts, vinegar.

5: Distilled water, pistachios, beef, coffee, white bread, wheat, nuts, peanuts.

6: Fruit juices, fish, eggs, tea, cooked spinach, cooked beans, soy milk, lima beans, plums, barley cocoa, liver, oyster, salmon, coconut, oats.

7: Most tap water, most spring water, river water, sea water.

8: Apples, tomatoes, pineapple, bell peppers, cherries, radishes, olives, almonds, grapefruit, turnips, soybeans, peaches, corn, mushrooms, strawberries, apricots, bananas, wild rice.

9: Avocados, dates, papayas, tangerines, figs, mangoes, grapes, beets, kiwi, melons, pears, blueberries, sweet potatoes, green tea, lettuce, peas, eggplant, celery.

10: Spinach, collard greens, onions, kale, asparagus, seaweed, lemons, limes, carrot, cucumbers, Brussels Sprouts, artichoke, broccoli, cauliflower.

Inflammation

The key to fighting inflammation is to consume raw materials in your juice or foods that are anti-inflammatory.

There are spices and herbs below which have anti-inflammatory properties:

- Cinnamon
- Rosemary
- Oregano
- Basil
- Nutmeg
- Cloves
- Cayenne pepper
- Garlic turmeric
- Black pepper
- Ginger
- Chives
- Chamomile
- Cardamom

There are other anti-inflammatory ingredients that you might enjoy in your juices or foods, including:

- Cucumber
- Banana
- Celery
- Tomatoes
- Berries
- Whole grains
- Herring
- Kippers

- Salmon
- Pumpkin
- Peas
- Lentils
- String beans
- Beans
- Quinoa

As a rule of thumb, anti-inflammatory foods are high in polyphenols and contain a lot of omega-3. They are also high in fiber.

Cravings

As you make the change toward the vegan diet, your body might start to crave things. When you start to make dietary changes, you may need to test the waters a bit with different recipes and you might have to experience a learning curve before you can find meals and recipes that give you all of the nutrients you need and help to keep you energized. You may experience cravings at first which indicate that your body is not consuming enough. But you might also get a craving for another reason.

Your body will naturally crave things when it requires a particular nutrient and being able to recognize those cravings can enable you to incorporate whatever nutrient is missing into your next meal.

When you feel a deep crave for chocolate it means your body needs magnesium. When this happens try to incorporate the following into your next meal:

- Nuts
- Seeds
- Fruit
- Legumes

If your body is craving sweets or sugary foods it needs things such as Chromium, Phosphorous, Sulphur, Carbon, or Tryptophan. When this happens it is best to incorporate:

- Fresh fruit
- Broccoli
- Raisins
- Sweet potatoes
- Grapes
- Spinach
- Nuts

When you feel a deep crave for bread or pasta your body needs nitrogen. When this happens try to incorporate the following into your next meal:

- Beans
- Nuts

When you feel a deep crave for oily foods or fatty foods your body needs calcium. When this happens try to incorporate the following into your next meal

- Green leafy vegetables
- Broccoli

If you are overeating your body may need silicon or tyrosine so you should eat:

- Spinach
- Nuts
- Seeds
- Fruit
- Vegetables
- Raisins

Growing At Home

One of the easiest ways to transition into this diet is to start a small garden at home, even if you just have a standing greenhouse on a balcony or on a window sill. Growing a garden at home can save you so much time and money over the long run and will make it easier to maintain this healthier diet. Instead of having to hope that you can find the ingredients you need, free from any chemicals or additives, you can rest assured knowing that they are right there in your garden. You can stick to a whole food, plant based diet and enjoy the multiple benefits that are associated with tending a small garden. All you'll need to do is stock up on whole grains and then pick daily from your garden the items you want to include for your meals.

A full guide to growing foods at home would warrant another full book so I will simply highlight some of the best foods to grow at home and encourage you to do a little research! It's truly worth it, one of my favorite parts of the day is picking from my home mini-farm and consuming the foods right away, as fresh as can be.

Here is a list of the ten fruits, vegetables and herbs that I believe are the easiest to grow at home: Sweetcorn, peppers, tomatoes, zucchini, cilantro, basil and mint, all kinds of berries, kale and peas.

Chapter Three: Diet Plans

Creating a Diet Plan

When you make the switch to vegetarianism, you will want to create comprehensive meals that enable you to consume foods rich in nutrients. In doing so, you are able to create a diet plan that gives you wonderful results.

The 10 Super food groups to include in your

vegetarian diet

Leafy Greens:

Leafy greens include kale, chard, and spinach. You may prefer kale because it is high in flavonoids, carotenoids, antioxidants, Omega 3, fiber, vitamin K, calcium, folate, and iron. Spinach has twice the fiber as other greens and gives you folate, vitamin B1, B2, and B6, vitamin A, calcium, vitamin C, Omega 3, iron, niacin, phosphorus, beta-carotenes, and will reduce your blood pressure and help fight against heart disease and bone degeneration.

Berries:

Some of the most beneficial berries include; strawberries, raspberries, blueberries and goji berries. Berries have fructose in them, but your body needs this sugar in order to stay healthy. Blueberries have antioxidants, vitamins A, C, E, and K, fiber, zinc, calcium, manganese, lycopene, niacin, and will fight heart disease.

Quinoa:

Although it's usually referred to as a grain, it is actually a seed related to spinach and beets. It comes in a variety of colors and has two great selling points: it's gluten-free and it's a great, complete source of protein. Complete sources of protein are rare in the plant world, making quinoa an excellent source for vegans. It is high in iron and calcium as well as being a great source of manganese, magnesium, copper and fiber. It is really easy to cook, and also works great in a salad.

Amaranth:

Another gluten-free grain that is a great source of protein, folate and vitamin B6. It is a good source of fiber and is one of the few grains to contain the amino acid lysine. It is second only to quinoa in terms of iron content and it has been shown to reduce cholesterol levels. It is also one of the only grains to be a source of vitamin C!

Sweet potatoes:

These tubers are a wonderful source of vitamins and minerals. Rich in Vitamins A, C, D and B6 and full of minerals; potassium, iron and magnesium these potatoes will be a staple of your diet.

Kiwi:

These delicious, slightly sour fruits are proof that great things can come in small packages. One large kiwi can provide your entire recommended daily dosage of vitamin C by itself! They are full of vitamins A and E, vitamin E being a vitamin that vegans can sometimes become deficient in. I recommend that you eat at least a few of these a week.

Flax and Chia seeds:

These seeds are one the greatest sources of Omega-3 and 6 for a vegan. The other common option for consuming these fatty acids is fish oils, clearly not an option for us! Chia seeds are a good protein source as well as being full of calcium, potassium, fiber and vitamin B complex. Whilst flax seeds have been suggested to help fight cancer by inhibiting tumor growth and by reducing hormone metabolism.

Avocadoes:

As discussed earlier, the saturated fats of animals clog people's arteries. However the fats found in plant foods are good for our health. Avocadoes are a wonderful source of monosaturated fats, whilst also being full of potassium, folate and vitamins K and E. They are a lovely addition to most sandwiches or salads.

Spirulina and Chlorella:

Spirulina is a cyanobacteria that is now considered one of the most nutritious food sources on the planet! The United Nations World Food Conference called it "the best food for the future". It is a complete protein source rich in B vitamins and has been reported to help correct anemia and reduce radioactive damage and lower cholesterol. Chlorella is a similar green algae that acts as a detoxifier for the body. When combined these two algae's can have a profound effect on your health. Just beware of the taste, it can take some getting used to!

Almonds:

These nuts are crammed full of vitamins, healthy fats and fiber. Due to their high fat content they are very calorie dense, making them a perfect food for snacking on. They can also be used in oatmeal, desserts and salads. Be sure to carry a small bag of these with you wherever you go!

2 x 4-Week Meal Plans

Here you will find two sets of meal plans. One is for vegetarians who avoid all animal meat and one is for vegetarians who still consume fish. These don't need to be followed religiously, be sure to experiment and change things around. Most of the meals listed in the diet plan are recipes provided in the later chapters. A few of the meals do not have a specific recipe, for example "Big salad using Romaine lettuce", in this case I will leave it up to you to knock up a quick meal! Be sure to choose two snacks from the snack recipe chapter each day to consume when you are feeling peckish or are in need of an energy boost!

Meal Plan #1: For Non-Fish Eaters

Week 1

Monday
Breakfast: Two eggs and potatoes
Lunch: Big salad using Romaine lettuce
Dinner: Black beans, wild rice and sliced apples

Tuesday
Breakfast: Fresh strawberry and banana smoothie
Lunch: Mixed vegetables and rice
Dinner: Stuffed bell peppers and avocado

Wednesday
Breakfast: Spinach and onion omelet with avocado
Lunch: Grilled chickpeas and cauliflower with asparagus
Dinner: Black bean salad with spinach and romaine lettuce

Thursday
Breakfast: Potato scramble with hot chili sauce
Lunch: Tofu patty and spinach
Dinner: Beans, rice and mashed cauliflower

Friday
Breakfast: Green smoothie with kale and kiwi
Lunch: salad with an apple
Dinner: Grilled vegetable kebabs

Saturday

Breakfast: Two eggs and Greek yogurt with berries
Lunch: Sautéed onions and carrots with sweet potatoes
Dinner: Tofu burger patty with steamed vegetables

Sunday
Breakfast: Pancakes with blueberries or with strawberries
Lunch: Steamed vegetables and wild rice
Dinner: Stuffed squash with mixed berries

Week 2

Monday
Breakfast: Whole wheat toast with peanut butter and blueberries
Lunch: Spinach salad with nuts
Dinner: Vegetable taquitos and diced avocadoes

Tuesday
Breakfast: Green smoothie with spinach and peaches
Lunch: Steamed vegetables and wild rice
Dinner: Stuffed bell peppers with grilled asparagus and caramelized onions

Wednesday
Breakfast: Two eggs and potatoes
Lunch: Vegetable curry with basmati rice
Dinner: Grilled chickpea salad with spinach and romaine

Thursday
Breakfast: Pancakes with blueberries
Lunch: Black bean and rice lettuce wraps
Dinner: Stuffed squash with mixed berries

Friday
Breakfast: Potato scramble with hot chili sauce
Lunch: Vegetable curry with basmati rice
Dinner: Vegetable taquitos and diced avocadoes

Saturday
Breakfast: Sautéed vegetables including spinach and broccoli
Lunch: Spinach salad with zucchini
Dinner: Beans, rice and mashed cauliflower

Sunday
Breakfast: Whole wheat toast with peanut butter and blueberries
Lunch: Vegetable lo Mein with egg rolls
Dinner: Stuffed squash with applesauce from scratch

Week 3

Monday
Breakfast: Whole wheat toast with peanut butter and blueberries
Lunch: Tofu burger with carrots
Dinner: Coconut glazed sweet potato with rice

Tuesday
Breakfast: Two eggs and potatoes
Lunch: Cauliflower tacos
Dinner: Vegetable lo Mein with egg rolls

Wednesday
Breakfast: Pancakes with real honey
Lunch: Black bean-stuffed bell peppers
Dinner: Stir fry

Thursday
Breakfast: Banana and pear green smoothie
Lunch: Rice with steamed broccoli
Dinner: Vegetable chili with cornbread

Friday
Breakfast: 3 egg omelet
Lunch: Spinach salad with shrimp
Dinner: Vegetable lo Mein with egg rolls

Saturday
Breakfast: Breakfast omelet with sautéed spinach
Lunch: Strawberry spinach salad with romaine
Dinner: Vegetable curry with Pad Thai noodles

Sunday
Breakfast: pancakes with banana slices
Lunch: Vegetable burritos
Dinner: Cauliflower tacos

Week 4

Monday
Breakfast: Two eggs and garlic hash browns with kale
Lunch: Vegetable curry with Pad Thai noodles
Dinner: Tofu burger with carrots

Tuesday
Breakfast: Strawberries and bananas
Lunch: Vegetable chili with cornbread
Dinner: Vegetable lo Mein with egg rolls

Wednesday
Breakfast: Two eggs and potatoes
Lunch: Chickpea avocado salad
Dinner: Vegetable stew

Thursday
Breakfast: Whole wheat toast with peanut butter and blueberries
Lunch: Coconut glazed sweet potato with rice
Dinner: Vegetable curry with Pad Thai noodles

Friday
Breakfast: Green smoothie with kale and kiwi
Lunch: Vegetable lo Mein with egg rolls
Dinner: Vegetable curry with Pad Thai noodles

Saturday
Breakfast: Greek yogurt with berries and granola
Lunch: Vegetable curry with basmati rice
Dinner: Spinach potato tacos

Sunday
Breakfast: Pancakes with strawberries
Lunch: Salad with romaine lettuce
Dinner: Tofu burger with carrots

Meal Plan #2: For Fish Eaters

Week 1

Monday
Breakfast: Tofu sausage with sautéed spinach
Lunch: Vegetable chili with cornbread
Dinner: Vegetable curry with Pad Thai noodles

Tuesday
Breakfast: 3 egg omelet
Lunch: Coconut curry vegetable stir fry
Dinner: Cilantro, lime, chickpeas with tomato and cucumber salad

Wednesday
Breakfast: Greek yogurt with berries and granola
Lunch: Asian lettuce wrap with pineapple
Dinner: Salmon patties with spinach and romaine lettuce

Thursday
Breakfast: Two eggs and garlic hash browns with kale
Lunch: Tuna salad with an apple
Dinner: Green chili taco salad

Friday
Breakfast: Banana and pear green smoothie
Lunch: Tomato salad with hard boiled eggs
Dinner: Creamy tomato soup with almond bread

Saturday
Breakfast: Whole wheat toast + peanut butter and blueberries
Lunch: Egg salad rolled in lettuce
Dinner: Vegetable chili with cornbread

Sunday
Breakfast: Coconut pancakes with strawberries
Lunch: Coconut glazed sweet potato with rice
Dinner: Grilled potato with sautéed onions

Week 2

Monday
Breakfast: 3 egg omelet
Lunch: Shrimp and spinach salad
Dinner: Vegetable chili with cornbread

Tuesday
Breakfast: Assorted sautéed vegetables including spinach and broccoli
Lunch: Egg salad rolled in lettuce
Dinner: Vegetable curry with Pad Thai noodles

Wednesday
Breakfast: Eggs and garlic hash browns with kale
Lunch: Vegetable chili with cornbread
Dinner: Asian lettuce wrap with pineapple

Thursday
Breakfast: Greek yogurt with berries and granola
Lunch: Coconut curry stir fry
Dinner: Salmon with coleslaw

Friday
Breakfast: Green smoothie with kale and kiwi
Lunch: Vegetable curry with Pad Thai noodles
Dinner: Vegetable chili with cornbread

Saturday
Breakfast: Whole wheat toast with peanut butter and blueberries
Lunch: Tuna salad with almonds
Dinner: Vegetable chili with cornbread

Sunday
Breakfast: 3 egg onion and spinach omelet
Lunch: Vegetable chili with cornbread
Dinner: Coconut glazed sweet potato with rice

Week 3

Monday
Breakfast: Greek yogurt with berries and granola
Lunch: Coconut glazed sweet potato with rice
Dinner: Stuffed Peppers

Tuesday
Breakfast: Green smoothie with kale and kiwi
Lunch: Citrus salad stir fry
Dinner: Coconut glazed sweet potato with rice

Wednesday
Breakfast: Mixed nuts and berries
Lunch: Bean and broccoli salad
Dinner: Vegetable curry with Pad Thai noodles

Thursday
Breakfast: 3 egg and spinach omelet
Lunch: Lemon and garlic scallops
Dinner: Pumpkin chili

Friday
Breakfast: Pancakes with real honey
Lunch: Tuna salad with almonds and lettuce
Dinner: Tofu burger with sweet potato fries

Saturday
Breakfast: Breakfast omelet with sautéed spinach
Lunch: Zucchini with sweet potatoes
Dinner: Grilled trout with butternut squash soup

Sunday
Breakfast: Pancakes with blackberries
Lunch: Tuna salad with celery
Dinner: Vegetable curry with Pad Thai noodles

Week 4

Monday
Breakfast: Onion and spinach omelet
Lunch: Salad with roasted chickpeas and tomatoes
Dinner: Grilled salmon with mixed berries

Tuesday
Breakfast: Assorted sautéed vegetables including spinach and broccoli
Lunch: Shrimp and spinach salad
Dinner: Grilled trout with butternut squash

Wednesday
Breakfast: Breakfast omelet with sautéed spinach
Lunch: Black bean and corn cakes and sweet potatoes
Dinner: Vegetable curry with basmati rice

Thursday
Breakfast: Banana and pear green smoothie
Lunch: Vegetable soup
Dinner: Bean, rice, and avocado burritos and sliced apples

Friday
Breakfast: Fruit Salad with Cinnamon
Lunch: Vegetable curry with Pad Thai noodles
Dinner: Coconut glazed sweet potato with rice

Saturday
Breakfast: Pancakes with blueberries
Lunch: Mixed vegetables and nuts
Dinner: Salmon and avocado with salt

Sunday
Breakfast: Two eggs and garlic hash browns with kale
Lunch: Vegetarian stir fry and brown rice
Dinner: Tofu patty with steamed vegetables

Chapter Four: 10 Breakfast Recipes

Below you will find ten vegetarian recipes that you can use for your next meal. Make sure you try different whole food items and spices to find a flavor that best suits your taste!

Potato scramble with hot chili sauce

Ingredients:

- 1 ½ cup chopped red onion
- 3 tablespoons yellow mustard
- ½ teaspoon ground allspice
- 1 ½ teaspoon chopped jalapeno
- 1 cup water
- 2 pounds potatoes, cubed
- 5 finely chopped tomatoes
- ½ cup cilantro
- 3 tablespoons lime juice
- Whole grain tortillas or whole grain bread

You can prepare this dish up to two days ahead of time and leave it in your refrigerator, in an airtight container, until you are ready to serve it. When you are ready to serve, reheat.

Instructions:

- In a large skillet, combine chopped red onion, yellow mustard, ground allspice, chopped jalapeno, and water. Bring it to simmer. Cover the pot and cook until onions are translucent.
- Add potatoes cut into cubes and cook for five minutes on high heat. Reduce the heat to medium and cover, allowing the potatoes to cook until they are tender.
- Immediately before serving, stir in tomatoes, cilantro, and fresh lime juice. You can wrap this scramble in warm whole-grain tortillas, or you can toast six slices of whole-grain bread and distribute the scramble on top.

Garlic hash browns with kale

Ingredients:

- two large potatoes
- salt and pepper to taste
- six minced garlic cloves
- 1 cup shredded kale

Instructions:

- Preheat oven to 375°F.
- Shred potatoes and season to taste. Spread on a baking sheet and bake for 10 minutes.
- Remove them from the oven and toss them with minced garlic cloves and then pop them back onto your baking sheet. Cook them for another five minutes.
- While these are baking, sauté your shredded kale over medium heat with 1/8 inch of water and salt. Do not replenish your water as it starts to evaporate. Once your kale is soft, set it aside and allow it to cool.
- Season your shredded potatoes to your liking and top with your kale. You can even cover this delicious meal with your favorite salsa or dipping sauce.

Coconut Pancakes

Ingredients:

- 3 egg substitutes
- ¼ cup of coconut flour
- ½ teaspoon of baking powder
- ½ teaspoon of organic maple syrup
- Salt
- Berries
- Coconut Oil

Instructions:

- Whisk egg substitutes in a bowl, add coconut flour,
- baking powder,
- organic maple syrup and salt.
- Mix well, then mash berries into a bowl with one teaspoon of hot water. Heat coconut oil on a pan and cook pancake batter.

Scoop a helping of mashed berries on top and enjoy

Green smoothie with kiwi and kale

Ingredients:

- one cup of washed kale
- one kiwi with the skin peeled
- one cup of almond milk
- two tablespoons of honey
- one tray of ice

Instructions:

- Add kale, kiwi fruit, almond milk, honey and ice together in a blender. Mix on medium for a few minutes, pour into glass and serve.

Spinach and Onion Omelet

Ingredients:

- ½ cup spinach
- 1 small white onion diced
- 2 eggs
- Salt and pepper to taste

Instructions:

- Sautee diced onion and spinach until onion is golden. Add one teaspoon of water to help steam the spinach as you cook.
- Add eggs evenly over the mixture. Flip in half when the underside is cooked, and then flip it over to cook other side.
- Sprinkle with salt and pepper to taste, serve.

Whole Wheat Toast with Peanut Butter and Blueberries

Ingredients:

- One or two pieces of toast
- Peanut butter
- 1 handful of blueberries

Instructions:

- Toast the bread.
- Once done, spread evenly with a thick layer of peanut butter.
- Add handful of blueberries across the peanut butter and enjoy!

Banana and kiwi green smoothie

Ingredients:

- 1 banana peeled
- 1 kiwi peeled
- 1 ice tray
- 1 cup of almond milk

Instructions:

- Place kiwi and banana in your blender and blend until smooth.
- Add the almond milk and ice and bring it to a texture of your liking.

Greek yogurt with berries and granola

Ingredients:

- 1 cup of Greek yogurt
- ½ cup raspberries
- ½ cup blueberries
- ¼ cup granola

Instructions:

- Place Greek yogurt in a bowl, mix in the granola, top with berries and honey, serve and enjoy.

Over the Rainbow

Ingredients:

- 1 carrot
- Quarter of a cucumber
- 1 green apple
- A few slice of pear
- A squeeze of lemon juice
- A handful of spinach leaves
- A tiny chunk of ginger

Instructions:

- Mix all ingredients in the blender and enjoy!

Green Breakfast

Ingredients:

- 1 large green apple
- Half a cucumber
- 1 small carrot
- Quarter of a sweet green pepper
- 2 small cherry tomato
- A handful of green grapes
- A small handful of spinach

Instructions:

- Mix all ingredients in the blender and enjoy!

Chapter Five: 10 Lunch Recipes

Below you will find ten vegetarian lunch recipes that you can use for your next meal. Make sure you try different whole food items and spices to find a flavor that best suits your taste!

Tortilla soup

Ingredients:

- two large tomatoes
- 1 red bell pepper
- 1 green bell pepper
- 1 jalapeno pepper (de-seeded to reduce spice)
- one half yellow onion roughly chopped
- salt to taste
- 2 cups of water
- cilantro
- avocado
- corn tortilla chips

Instructions:

- Place the cilantro, peppers, tomatoes, onion, and salt and pepper to taste in the water. Allow to sit on medium heat for 45 minutes until the vegetables are tender.
- To serve, garnish with cilantro and avocado on top. Squeeze lemon juice lightly over the bowl and serve with your corn tortilla chips.

Chickpea and Broccoli Salad

Ingredients:

- 1 cup chickpeas
- ½ cup broccoli
- spinach
- salt and pepper

Instructions:

- Prepare chickpeas overnight in water and then prepare on the stove top, or use a can of chickpeas (appx. 16 ounces), rinsed.
- Prepare your broccoli (i.e. steamed or grilled) to taste.
- Add to your freshly washed spinach, and toss with chickpeas and broccoli. Season to taste.

Strawberry and almond salad

Ingredients:

- romaine lettuce
- spinach
- one cup of freshly diced strawberries
- ½ cup of roasted almonds

Instructions:

- Rinse and chop romaine lettuce and spinach.
- Add one cup of freshly diced strawberries.
- Add ½ cup of thinly sliced roasted almonds.
- Toss with coconut oil and enjoy!

Liquid Salad

Ingredients:

- Half a cucumber
- 2 tomatoes
- A squeeze of lemon juice
- Quarter of a red bell pepper
- Pinch of parsley
- A teaspoon of diced onion

Instructions:

- Mix all ingredients in the blender and enjoy!

Beet Nik

Ingredients:

- 2 carrots
- 1 red apple
- 1 cup of beetroot
- 2 celery stalks
- A handful of spinach

Instructions:

- Mix all ingredients in the blender and enjoy!

Vegetarian stir fry and brown rice

Ingredients:

- ½ cup sliced carrots
- 1 diced bell pepper
- ½ cup broccoli florets
- 1 small white onion diced
- 2 tablespoons olive oil
- 1 cup brown rice

Instructions:

- Heat olive oil in pan.
- Add all of the vegetables and season to taste. Cook until the vegetables become tender.
- Prepare the brown rice as per the instructions.
- Serve with the stir fry on top of the rice and enjoy!

Vegetable curry with Pad Thai noodles

Ingredients:

- 1 small white onion
- ½ cup dice carrots
- ½ cup broccoli florets
- 1 small Yukon potato diced
- 1 cup snap peas
- 2 tablespoons olive oil
- 1 package pad Thai noodles
- 1 package curry seasoning

Instructions:

- Sauté the vegetables in olive oil.
- Prepare the pad Thai noodles in hot water, as per instructions.
- Prepare the curry seasoning as per the instructions. If you have curry powder, add to water until you have achieved the texture you desire.
- When the vegetables are soft, mix with the curry sauce and allow to simmer for 15 minutes.
- Serve with the pad Thai noodles.

Vegetable chili

Ingredients:

- 2 medium sweet potatoes
- 1 teaspoon cayenne pepper
- 1 teaspoon cumin
- 1 teaspoon cinnamon
- 1 cup black beans
- 1 cup kidney beans
- 1 cup chopped tomatoes
- 1 fresh red chili
- 1 cup fresh coriander
- 1 red pepper
- 1 yellow pepper
- 1 large onion (color of your choice)
- Olive oil
- Salt and pepper to taste

Instructions:

- Pre-heat the oven to 400°F
- Peel the sweet potatoes and dice. Cover with cayenne pepper, cumin, and cinnamon. Drizzle with olive oil.
- Bake potatoes for 40 minutes.
- Meanwhile, sauté onion, de-seeded chili pepper, and bell peppers for 10 minutes until soft.
- Drain the beans and bring them to boil in the pan with the onion and pepper mixture. Add the tomatoes and the tomato juice from the can. Add the coriander and bring to a boil, then reduce heat to medium and cook for 25 minutes while adding one teaspoon of water at a time as necessary to reduce the thickness.
- Stir in the potatoes when done and season with salt and pepper.

Shrimp and Spinach Salad

Ingredients:

- 1/2 cup shrimp
- 1 cup spinach
- 1 tablespoon feta cheese
- Olive oil to taste

Instructions:

- Prepare shrimp as desired.
- Wash and pat dry spinach.
- Mix with shrimp and sprinkle with feta cheese.
- Enjoy!

Fresh Arugula Salad Pizza

Ingredients:

- Whole grain pizza dough
- 1/3 cup marinara sauce
- 1 teaspoon dried oregano
- 1 cup shredded cheese
- 2 cups fresh arugula and baby spinach
- 1 cup fresh cherry tomatoes, cut in half
- ½ medium red bell pepper diced
- 1 tablespoon balsamic vinegar
- 1 tablespoon olive oil

Instructions:

- Preheat your oven to 350°F.
- Roll out the pizza dough and spread the marinara sauce on top. Sprinkle the dough with the cheese and oregano.
- Place the dough into the oven for 30 minutes until the crust is golden.
- Top the crust with the rest of the ingredients before serving and drizzle with olive oil and vinegar.
- Serve immediately and enjoy.

Chapter Six: 10 Dinnertime Recipes

Below you will find ten vegetarian dinner time recipes that you can use for your next meal. Make sure you try different whole food items and spices to find a flavor that best suits your taste!

Vegetable Lasagna

Ingredients:

- 1 cup spinach
- 1 diced eggplant
- 1 cup tomato sauce
- 1 diced bell pepper
- Lasagna pasta
- 1 tablespoon olive oil
- 1 cup Mozzarella cheese
- ½ cup parmesan cheese
- 1 cup ricotta cheese
- 1 egg

Instructions:

- Bring water to boil with 1 tablespoon olive oil.
- Place in lasagna pasta pieces and allow to cook until slightly tender.
- Remove each piece and place on a sheet of aluminum foil, without touching. Allow to cool.
- In the meantime, cover the diced eggplant and peppers with salt, pepper, and a dish of olive oil. Cook for 15 minutes at 350°F.
- Mix parmesan cheese with ricotta cheese and egg.
- Prepare the layers of your lasagna to your liking including the eggplant, bell pepper, sauce, spinach, ricotta mixture, and mozzarella cheese.
- Cover with foil and bake at 350°F for 40 minutes until the cheese on top is bubbling slightly.

Vegetable Soup

Ingredients:

- one large chopped onion
- two large chopped carrots
- two large chopped celery stocks
- 1 to 2 tablespoons of water
- three minced garlic cloves
- 1 tablespoon grated ginger
- 1 1/2 tablespoons of sweet paprika
- 2 tablespoons ground cumin
- 1 tablespoon of ground coriander
- 2 1-inch pieces of cinnamon stick
- 8 cups of vegetable stock or a low sodium vegetable broth
- one medium butternut squash, cubed
- one turnip, cubed
- one potato, cubed
- 18 ounces of crushed tomatoes
- 2 cups of cooked chickpeas.
- two large pinches of saffron
- 2 tablespoons of freshly chopped mint
- cilantro

Instructions:

- Soak saffron in 1/4 cup of warm water.

Place onion, carrots, and celery sticks into a large pot and sauté them for 10 minutes. Add water slowly to prevent them from sticking to your pan. Then add garlic cloves, grated ginger, sweet Paprika, ground cumin, ground coriander and cinnamon stick, and cook for three minutes.

- Add vegetable stock or a low sodium vegetable broth, cubed butternut squash, turnip, and potato, crushed tomatoes and chickpeas. Bring this to a boil over high heat.

- Reduce the heat to simmer and cook for 25 minutes uncovered.
- Add soaked saffron and mint. Season your stew with salt and pepper and cook for 10 minutes or until your vegetables are tender.
- Top with finely chopped cilantro and serve.

Black bean burritos

Ingredients:

- one large yellow onion
- 1 tablespoon of water
- four cloves of minced garlic
- 2 teaspoons of ground cumin seeds
- two chilies or 2 teaspoons of chili powder
- 2 to 3 cups of prepared black bean
- 18 corn tortillas

Instructions:

- Sauté onion in a saucepan for 10 minutes. Continually add 1 tablespoon of water at a time to keep them from sticking to the pan. Add minced garlic and cook for one minute. Add ground cumin seeds and two chilies or chili powder. Add black beans and season, then puree until smooth.
- Place 18 corn tortillas in a nonstick skillet over medium heat and heat them until they are soft. Spread 3 tablespoons of your black bean mixture over each and roll them. Once you have prepared all of your tortillas, serve with the delicious tomato salsa.

Cauliflower Tacos

Ingredients:

- 1 medium head cauliflower
- 2 tablespoons olive oil
- ½ teaspoon salt
- 1 can chickpeas
- ½ teaspoon salt
- ¼ teaspoon chilli powder
- ¼ teaspoon cumin
- 2 cups fresh cilantro
- 1 garlic clove
- 8 tortillas

Instructions:

- Pre-heat your oven to 425°F.
- Cut the cauliflower into florets and drizzle in a bowl with salt and olive oil until evenly covered. Place on a cookie sheet and bake for 15 minutes until browned. At the same time, mix the chickpeas with salt, chilli powder and cumin. Drizzle with olive oil and bake for 15 minutes until browned.
- Spoon the cilantro and garlic onto the tortillas and top with 1 teaspoon of chickpeas and ½ cup of florets. Garnish with lime juice and serve.

Stuffed Peppers

Ingredients:

- one bell pepper
- black beans
- 1 small jalapeno, deseeded and finely chopped
- one glove of garlic
- one tablespoon of cinnamon
- 1 tablespoon of cumin.
- one cup of wild rice or brown rice
- cilantro
- avocado strips
- vegetables of your choice for stuffing

Instructions:

- Wash and cut bell pepper in half.
- Remove any seeds and stem.
- Prepare black beans with chopped jalapeno, garlic, cinnamon, and cumin.
- Prepare one cup of wild rice or brown rice and mix with cilantro.
- Add rice, beans, and other vegetable you wish to the bell peppers.
- Top with avocado strips, serve and enjoy!

Tasty Bean Burgers

Ingredients:

- 1 large minced onion
- 1 minced garlic
- 1 tablespoon of paprika
- 1 teaspoon of cayenne pepper
- ¼ teaspoon of sea salt
- ¼ cup of almond meal
- 2 eggs
- ¼ teaspoon of pepper
- 1 pound black beans, prepared and mashed
- Buns and toppings for burgers

Instructions:

- Preheat your oven to 300°F.
- Cook onion and garlic in a pan on medium heat until they are soft.
- Mix the onion and garlic in a bowl with paprika, cayenne pepper, sea salt, almond meal, eggs and pepper. Form inch-thick patties with mashed black beans and cook in a pan until brown on both sides, then cover in mixture and place in the oven for 25 minutes.
- Assemble burgers and serve.

Pasta with Roasted Vegetables

Ingredients:

- 8 ounces of whole wheat penne pasta
- 1 eggplant cut into small chunks
- 1 red bell pepper diced
- 4 cups broccoli florets
- 2 tablespoons olive oil
- 4 sliced garlic cloves
- 1/3 cup sundried tomatoes
- 1/3 cup pitted Kalamata olives
- 1 tablespoon balsamic vinegar

Instructions:

- Preheat your oven to 425°F and line a roasting pan with baking parchment
- Combine the onion, garlic, and broccoli in a bowl and drizzle with olive oil. Place in the roasting pan and gently mix with the other vegetables.
- Place in the oven and cook for 20 minutes until the vegetables are roasted.
- Prepare the pasta al dente and drain.
- Take the vegetables out of the oven and add the dried tomatoes, olives, and balsamic vinegar.
- Toss together and serve.

Pinto Bean and Quinoa Sloppy Joes

Ingredients:

- ½ cup quinoa
- 1 tablespoon olive oil
- 1 medium yellow onion chopped
- ½ green bell pepper diced
- 1 ½ cup pinto beans drained and rinsed
- 1 can of tomato sauce
- 1 medium diced tomato
- 1 tablespoon soy sauce
- 2 teaspoons chilli powder
- 1/2 teaspoon paprika
- 1/4 teaspoon dried oregano
- Whole grain rolls

Instructions:

- Combine quinoa with 1 cup of water and bring to boil. Reduce heat, cover and allow to simmer for 15 minutes.
- Heat the olive oil and in a skillet and sauté the onion. Add the bell pepper and sauté until both are tender. Add the rest of the ingredients, except rolls, and heat over medium heat for 5 minutes. Allow the mixture to stand for five minutes. Add the quinoa and let it soak up the flavour for another five minutes.
- Spoon the mixture over your rolls and serve with a salad or corn on the cob.

Smokey Bean Burgers

Ingredients:

- 1/3 cup quick cook oats
- ½ cup sunflower seeds
- 1 can pinto beans drained and rinsed
- ½ green bell pepper diced
- ½ cup hemp seeds
- 2 teaspoons salt
- 1 teaspoon chilli powder
- 1 teaspoon paprika powder
- 1 tablespoon olive oil
- Salt and pepper to taste
- Whole grain buns
- Lettuce leaves and/or sliced tomatoes
- Your favorite condiments

Instructions:

- Preheat your oven to 400°F.
- Combine the oats in 2/3 cup boiling water.
- Grind the sunflower seeds until chopped coarsely. Add the beans, hemp seeds, bell pepper, seasonings, and olive oil. Evenly chop the mixture by hand or in a food processor. Add the sunflower seeds and oatmeal.
- Line a baking sheet and coat the inside of a measuring cup with olive oil.
- Spoon the mixture into the measuring cup, packing firmly then invert the patties to the parchment and flatten.
- Bake for 15 minutes, flip and bake for another 15 minutes.
- Serve with the bread and condiments of your choosing. Add smoked paprika to taste.

Pad Thai Noodles with Peanut Sauce

Ingredients:

- 1 package rice noodles
- 1 cup coconut milk
- ½ cup peanut butter
- 1 tablespoon fresh ginger
- 2 garlic cloves
- ½ teaspoon salt
- ¼ cup lime juice
- ½ teaspoon peanut oil
- 1 teaspoon chilli sauce
- 1 cup tofu
- 2 cups shiitake mushrooms sliced
- 1 red bell pepper diced
- 1 cup broccoli florets
- 1 cup snow peas
- 1 cup baby bok choy chopped
- ½ cup roasted peanuts
- Olive oil

Instructions:

- Prepare noodles according to the instructions.
- Mix coconut milk, peanut butter, ginger, garlic cloves, salt, lime juice, peanut oil, and chilli sauce. Blend and set aside.
- Heat 1tsp olive oil in pan and cook tofu until browned on all sides. Remove and set aside.
- Heat 1tsp olive oil and sauté shiitake mushrooms, bell pepper, broccoli florets, and snow peas for 10 minutes.
- Add baby bok choy and tofu, and cook for 2 minutes.
- Serve over rice noodles and garnish with roasted peanuts.

Chapter Seven: 10 Snack Recipes

Below you will find ten vegetarian recipes that you can use for your next snack. Make sure you try different whole food items and spices to find a flavor that best suits your taste!

Hummus

Ingredients:

- 15 ounces of prepared chickpeas
- two large garlic cloves
- 2 tablespoons of lemon juice
- black pepper and salt
- 1 tablespoon of cumin
- zest of one lemon
- One half teaspoon of ground turmeric.

Instructions:

- For the hummus, combine 15 ounces of prepared chickpeas with two large garlic cloves, 2 tablespoons of lemon juice, black pepper and salt to taste, and 1 tablespoon of cumin. Process this until it is smooth.

Coleslaw

Ingredients:

- 1 tablespoon of olive oil
- 1 teaspoon of raw honey
- 1/2 teaspoon of salt
- 1/2 teaspoon of pepper
- 1/2 teaspoon of ground mustard seed
- 1/8 teaspoon of cumin seed
- 2 tablespoons of apple cider vinegar
- 1 small red cabbage

Instructions:

- Mix olive oil, raw honey, salt, pepper, ground mustard seed, cumin seed, apple cider vinegar in a large bowl. Shred red cabbage and place in a separate bowl
- Add dressing to the cabbage and mix.
- Serve immediately.

Strawberry-Mint Delight

Ingredients:

- 2 cups pineapple
- 1 pear
- 1 cup strawberries
- Dash of peppermint

Instructions:

- Mix all ingredients in the blender and enjoy!

Red Dawn

Ingredients:

- 1 cup mango
- Quarter of a cucumber
- 1 small red apple
- 1 small carrot
- A handful of strawberries
- A red cabbage leaf
- Pinch of parsley

Instructions:

- Mix all ingredients in the blender and enjoy!

Fresh Salsa

Ingredients:

- 2 tomatoes
- 1 sweet green bell pepper
- 2 stalks of celery
- Pinch of cilantro
- Pinch of diced onion
- Pinch of diced garlic
- Dash of Cayenne Pepper
- Dash of salt

Instructions:

- Mix all ingredients in the blender and enjoy!

Pomegranate Delight

Ingredients:

- 2 pomegranates
- 1 green apple
- Handful of red grapes
- 2 celery stalks
- Quarter of a cucumber
- Handful of spinach

Instructions:

- Mix all ingredients in the blender and enjoy!

Tropical Alkaline Breeze

Ingredients:

- 1 young Thai coconut
- 8 carrots
- 2 celery stalks

Instructions:

- Mix all ingredients in the blender and enjoy!

Refreshing Green Energy

Ingredients:

- 7 Kale leaves
- Handful of basil
- 1 cucumber
- 2 stalks Fennel
- 4 large carrots
- 1 ginger knuckle

Instructions:

- Mix all ingredients in the blender and enjoy!

The Green Cooler

Ingredients:

- 3 ounces fresh wheatgrass juice
- Juice from 1 coconut
- 1 large cucumber

Instructions:

- Mix all ingredients in the blender and enjoy!

Golden Juice

Ingredients:

- 4 celery stalks
- 2 carrots
- 1 pear
- Half a cucumber
- Half a cup of beetroot
- Sprinkle of diced ginger

Instructions:

- Mix all ingredients in the blender and enjoy!

Chapter Eight: 10 Sauce, Dip and Condiments Recipes

Below you will find ten recipes that you can use to create vegan friendly sauces, dips and condiments. Make sure you try different whole food items and spices to find a flavor that best suits your taste!

Vegetarian Hummus

Ingredients:
- 2 cups of chickpeas
- Teaspoon of fresh lemon juice
- 3 tablespoon olive oil
- 3 tablespoons of water
- 1 garlic clove, minced
- 3 tablespoons of tahini
- ½ teaspoon of cumin
- Salt and pepper to taste

Instructions:

- Simply place all of the ingredients into a blender and blend until as smooth as possible. You may need to add additional water to achieve the right smoothness. Be sure to experiment with this recipe and try sprinkling in some paprika or olive oil before serving.

Broccoli Guacamole

Ingredients:
- 1 cup of broccoli, as finely chopped as possible
- 2 diced avocadoes
- 1 diced tomato
- ¼ cup of minced red onion
- 1 clove of garlic
- 1 tablespoon of lemon juice
- Cilantro
- Salt to taste

Instructions:
- Mix all of the ingredients together, except for the avocadoes.
- Gently fold the avocado chunks into the mixture
- Season with a tiny amount of salt, if needed.

Rocket and Cashew Spread

Ingredients:
- 1.5 cups raw cashew nuts
- 1 clove of garlic
- 2 cups of rocket
- ¼ cup of nutritional yeast
- 2 tablespoons of lemon juice
- ¼ cup of extra virgin olive oil
- Salt and pepper to taste

Instructions:
- Place the cashew nuts, nutritional yeast and a clove of garlic into a food processor and pulse it gently until the ingredients are all mixed but the cashews are still chunky. Place into a bowl and set aside.
- Blend the olive oil and lemon juice, followed by the rocket and then mix this mixture into the cashew mixture.
- Season with salt and pepper.
- Serve with crostini type crackers!

Vegetarian Pesto

Ingredients:
- ½ cup of lightly toasted pine nuts
- 2 cups of fresh basil
- ½ cup of extra virgin olive oil
- 1 clove of garlic, minced
- 2 teaspoons of lemon juice
- Salt and pepper to taste

Instructions:
- Blend all of the ingredients together in a food processor or immersion blender.
- Serve immediately.
- Can be frozen for up to 3 months

Cashew Mayonnaise

Ingredients:
- 2 tablespoons of flaxseed oil
- 2 tablespoons of extra virgin olive oil
- 1 cup of raw cashew nuts
- ¼ cup of water
- ¼ cup of fresh lemon juice
- 2 soft pitted medjool dates
- 1 teaspoon of salt
- 1 teaspoon of onion powder
- ½ teaspoon of garlic powder
- Pinch of ground black pepper

Instructions:
- Soak the cashew nuts for 2 hours and then drain.
- Combine the cashew nuts, water, salt and pepper, garlic and onion powder, dates and lemon juice in a blender and blend until smooth.
- Add the extra virgin olive oil and the flaxseed oil to the mixture and blend until emulsified.
- If you find the mixture becomes too thick, add a teaspoon of water at a time until it softens up.

Creamy Cauliflower Herb Salad Dressing

Ingredients:
- 1 cup of raw cauliflower florets
- 1 cup of water
- The juice of one whole lemon, 2 tablespoons worth
- 1 clove of garlic, peeled and minced
- 2 teaspoons of extra virgin olive oil
- 2 teaspoons of agave nectar
- 1 teaspoon of brown mustard
- 1 teaspoon of apple cider vinegar
- Salt and pepper to taste
- 2 tablespoons of fresh basil

Instructions:
- Roast the garlic with oil at a low temperature until the garlic is soft in a small frying pan.
- Put the cauliflower and water together in a pot and bring to boil. Cover and cook the cauliflower at a low temperature until it is tender. This should take roughly ten minutes.
- Chop up the basil.
- Add the contents of the pot into a blender and add the roasted garlic, lemon juice, mustard, apple cider vinegar, agave nectar. Add the salt and pepper to taste.
- Blend until creamy and smooth. Add a teaspoon or two of water if needed.
- Goes perfectly with a spinach salad.

Mango Chutney

Ingredients:
- ¼ teaspoon of curry powder
- 2 teaspoons of peanut oil
- 2 cloves of garlic, minced
- 2 tablespoons of red wine vinegar
- 2 teaspoons of grated ginger
- 2 tablespoons of water
- 1 seeded and chopped jalapeno
- 2 tablespoons of sugar or an alternative
- 1 large mango cut into small chunks

Instructions:
- Preheat a small saucepan over a low heat
- Place the oil, ginger, garlic and jalapeno in the pan and sauté for just around 90 seconds.
- Add the mango chunks, sugar and water.
- Turn the heat up to a medium temperature. Cover the saucepan and cook for 3 minutes, until it is boiling.
- Add the red wine vinegar and the curry powder, cook for a further minute without the lid.
- Allow to cool, stir for 5 minutes and the serve with any Indian meal.

Vegetarian BBQ Sauce

Ingredients:
- 1 cup of low sodium ketchup
- 3 tablespoons of barley malt syrup
- 1 teaspoon of Dijon mustard
- 3 tablespoons of water
- 2 tablespoons of extra virgin olive oil
- ½ teaspoon of garlic powder
- ¼ teaspoon of liquid smoke
- 1 ½ teaspoons of raw apple cider vinegar
- 1 teaspoon of Chile powder

Instructions:
- Simply whisk all of the ingredients together in a bowl until thoroughly mixed. Serve immediately!

Tzatziki Sauce

Ingredients:
- 1 medium sized cucumber, peeled and sliced in half.
- A pinch of cayenne pepper
- 2 cups of vegan mayonnaise
- 2 tablespoons of fresh mint
- ¼ cup of fresh lemon juice
- A pinch of ground black pepper
- 1 tablespoon of fresh dill
- 5 cloves of garlic, minced

Instructions:
- Grate the cucumber on a cheese graters' large holes.
- Combine the cucumber with the rest of the ingredients in a large bowl and mix thoroughly.
- Serve right away!

Cashew Hollandaise Sauce

Ingredients:
- 1/3 cup of soaked cashews
- 1 teaspoon of agave nectar
- 2 tablespoons of nutritional yeast
- 1 tablespoon of fresh lemon juice
- 1 teaspoon of mustard
- 1/3 cup of water
- 1/3 cup of unsweetened almond milk
- 1 tablespoon of extra virgin olive oil
- 1 teaspoon of apple cider vinegar
- A pinch of salt and pepper to taste

Instructions:
- Soak the cashew nuts for an hour in warm water.
- Drain and combine the cashews with the other ingredients in a blender.
- Blend until smooth
- Place the sauce in a saucepan and heat at a low temperature.
- Stir it with a whisk until thickened, add more water if it becomes too thick.
- Serve hot with steamed vegetables!

Conclusion

Thanks again for choosing this book, I truly hope it was able to help you begin your vegetarian journey. The health benefits are really quite impressive, particularly if coming from a diet rich in animal products. You will be reducing the chances of suffering from a whole myriad of diseases and conditions in the future. Not to mention doing your part in developing and protecting the rights of animals.

It's true, the vegetarian diet can be quite daunting to begin with. There is a lot to be aware of and for most it's a major lifestyle change. Just be sure to take it slow and ease into it. You are bound to make a couple of mistakes here and there, every vegan does! Don't get down about it, accept the mistake and keep on trucking. Over time you will find that following the principles of the diet becomes second nature.

I hope you found some inspiration in the recipes I have provided for you. Be sure to try them out and experiment over time with some additional or different flavors. People will often say that the vegetarian diet is boring and repetitive. This couldn't be further from the truth, all you need is a desire to experiment!

If you have enjoyed this book, then please be sure to leave a review for it!

Thanks and good luck with your vegan journey!
Jessica

Free Ebook Offer

The Ultimate Guide to Vitamins

I'm very excited to offer you a wonderful 10k word ebook that has been made available to you through my publisher, Valerian Press. As a health-conscious person, you should be well-aware of the uses and health benefits of each of the vitamins that should make up our diet. This book gives you an easy to understand scientific explanation of the vitamin, followed by the recommended daily dosage. It then highlights all the important health benefits of each vitamin. A list of the best sources of each vitamin is provided, and you are also given some actionable next steps to make sure you are utilizing the information!

As well as receiving the free ebook, you will also be sent a weekly stream of free ebooks from my publishing company Valerian Press. You can expect to receive at least one free ebook every week. Sometimes you might receive a massive 10 free books in a week!

All you need to do is simply type this link into your browser: http://bit.ly/18hmup4

About the Author

Hello! I'm Jessica Brooks, relatively new to the world of authorship but a veteran of the health and diet industry. If you have read any of my books, I would like to thank you from the bottom of my heart. I truly hope they have helped answer your questions and injected some inspiration into your life. Thanks to my wonderful upbringing I have been a vegetarian since infancy, making to jump to veganism nearly 20 years ago. I'm passionate about helping people improve their health! Over the coming months I am hoping to write a couple more books that will help people learn, start and succeed with certain diets.

In my spare time I am an avid reader of fantasy fiction (George Martin, you demon!). You can often find me lounging in my hammock with my latest book well into the evening. Outside of reading, I love all things physical. From hiking to sailing, swimming to skiing I'm a fan of it all! I try to practice Yoga a couple of times a week, I really recommend everyone gives it a try. You will just feel amazing after a good session!

You can find a facebook page I help manage here:

https://www.facebook.com/CleanFoodDiet

I would like to thank my publishers Valerian Press for giving me the opportunity to create this book.

Valerian Press

At Valerian Press we have three key beliefs.

Providing outstanding value: We believe in enriching all of our customers' lives, doing everything we can to ensure the best experience.

Championing new talent: We believe in showcasing the worlds emerging talent by giving them the platform to grow.

Simplicity and efficiency: We understand how valuable your time is. Our products are stream-lined and consist only of what you want. You will find no fluff with us.

We hope you have enjoyed reading Jessica's guide to the vegetarian diet.

We would love to offer you a regular supply of our free and discounted books. We cover a huge range of non-fiction genres; diet and cookbooks, health and fitness, alternative and holistic medicine, spirituality and plenty more

All you need to do is simply type this link into your browser: http://bit.ly/18hmup4

Printed in Great Britain
by Amazon.co.uk, Ltd.,
Marston Gate.